YOU TOO CAN BOUNCE BACK

You too can Bounce Back

---

10 STEPS TO SUCCESSFULLY NAVIGATE DISRUPTION

Nivarti Jayaram

Kolachalam Nagamaheswari

Acknowledgement

The book would not have been possible without
constant support and prodding from my better half, Bhavana,
who has been with me through all my successes and failures,
always motivating me to look at my next milestone rather than
just sitting on my laurels.
Thanks to my sons, Kaustubhasai and Vishwas, who have
been challenging and pushing me to put in all the effort
needed.
Special thanks to Mithra Gopalakrishna, Gaurav Agarwal, and
Anu Ravi and my close-knit group of friends (we call ourselves
the "GPS") who have been pillars of support in my journey

I must thank my esteemed Coach and Mentor Mr.
Anant Krishnan for providing his valuable feedback on the
way I have shared my experiences through the book especially
the Introduction.

1

INTRODUCTION

Disruption is no longer an exception but a norm. With the onset of COVID in 2020, the level of disruption has only magnified exponentially with most organizations forced to move towards remote working. The disruption has also impacted most small to medium sized organizations and has compelled them to alter their vision & strategies. This has resulted in many losing their livelihood and earning capacity impacting their near & dears apart from themselves.

Even for those who still are in the comfort of their workplace, there is a lot of uncertainty about their careers and its security which leads to anxiety and disturbs the way they are going about their lives. The impact is to their physical, mental, and emotional health which cascades to their immediate circle of influence too (Family & extended ones).

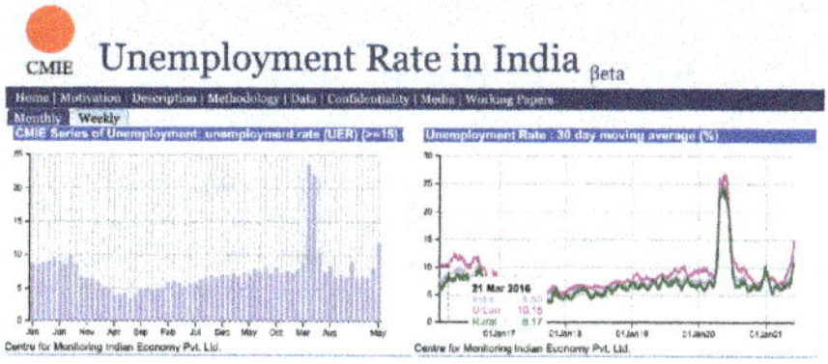

As per Centre for Managing Indian Economy's report, the country saw a job loss of close to 10 Million and the overall % of job loss peaked to 24.5% during Jun 2020 in the first wave of COVID & again peaked to 11.33% in Jun 2021 in the second wave of COVID.

The job loss % has been almost same across both Rural & Urban areas with Urban contributing 26% as against 23% by Rural areas to the overall numbers In Jun 2020. The contribution by Rural areas is more than 10% as against Urban areas being more than 13% in the second wave in Jun 2021.

With such a huge increase in job loss, it becomes increasingly difficult to get reemployed until unless you have the right level of expertise, credentials, and a strong personal & professional network to bank on. The question then that remains is, what should the rest of the people who are impacted be looking at? How can they earn their livelihood, continue to fulfil their responsibilities, and cater for their future needs? What options or opportunities they have for them to look up to? How can they overcome the personal & social stigma and emerge stronger through the situation? These are the questions that we look to answer through the rest of the book.

Loss of earning capacity and the compelling demands of life collectively create a sense of despair for individuals. People who lost their jobs or potentially looking at job loss are largely influenced by their current standards of life. Usually, when everything is going well in life, we don't think about creating sustenance plans and when things go wrong, we won't have time to do so.

While many of those impacted might be ready to compromise their own standard of living, they look to maintain the same style & standard of living for their immediate family members. This means, whatever savings they would have, they spend it towards maintaining the life style which they are used to, even when the earning situation is not the same it once used to be. Some compelled by their love & affection to their families and others compelled by the fear of society.

COVID is not the only reason due to which we might be looking at a job loss or potential job loss scenario. There are a number of other reasons that could result in a similar situation. Few of those are:

Global Recession: Few from the current generation may be aware of the global recession that disrupted world's most economies in 2008.

The recession led to loss of numerous jobs as the financial industry collapsed triggering widespread impact to all other sectors. Lots of companies had to either close or scale down their operations considerably to manage the impact. While US could recover by 2009, the impact was experiences in many other countries for a much longer period.

- War: We don't need a war to start between two countries for the economies to be disrupted, even a potential war scenario could trigger the collapse of economies leading to various industry sectors getting impacted, especially those established to fulfil offshored service needs. This again leads to potential job losses are organizations become conservative and look reduce their operational expenditure.
- Terrorism: Continued & sustained acts of terrorism in a particular country can cause disruption as the developed countries

and major industry leading organizations would either withdraw their current investments or stop any potential investments planned. This also can lead to existing jobs to cease and /or influence future job creation.

- Business Sector: Depending on how the overall sentiments are in a particular business sector and also the spending capabilities of a country citizens, specific business sectors could be impacted. For ex: Aviation Sector in India has been in crisis for a long time now and has resulted in two major Airline Operators (Kingfisher & Jet Airways) going out of business. It also had cascaded impact on their business partners from beyond Aviation Sector. This resulted in impacting thousands of skilled people and their immediate families not just in India but across the globe.
- Acquisition: Sale, Mergers & Acquisition of companies is part of business strategy. However, every sale or acquisition leads to lot of job losses. The quantum of impact is driven by the reasons for which the strategies are being executed. For ex: Dell acquired EMC in 2016 to facilitate Dell to become one stop shop for their existing as well as potential business customers. This is a capability extension strategy which usually doesn't lead to major job losses. However, you would still see impact to leadership & executive positions due to duplication of roles, consolidation of capabilities etc. Acquisition & Merger of rival companies targeting similar business sectors can lead to greater job losses due to the existence of similar capabilities in both the acquiring & acquired organization. IBM acquiring RedHat could be a possible example to look at. (The examples quoted are only for reference)
- Emerging Technologies: Technology evolution is another one of the major disruptors across industries. The pace of evolution is much higher than the pace at which they are learned & consumed. An individual or organization needs to be smart enough, connected to the latest developments around their capabilities and have futuristic vision to continue to excel. If not, then the fight is always for survival, and we will be losing the game one

day of the other. Continuous learning is the key to sustain & excel through rapid & dynamic the technology evolution.

Classic examples of major companies that went out of business because they couldn't foresee technology disruptions are KODAK & NOKIA. The impact these have had are well known from their history.

- Start-ups: Start-ups address specific business problems for the customers and have the capability to disrupt even the well-established organizations with their business models. One of the examples is Airbnb.

"Air Bed and Breakfast", popularly known as Airbnb came up with a business model where they provided a platform for hosts to accommodate guests with short-term lodging and tourism-related activities. This hugely impacted the hotel industry as their business model made travel stay more affordable and also proved beneficial for owners of residences & apartments.

- Leadership Change: Leadership change, especially at the top can lead to big changes in Organizational strategies & structure. This has a direct cascading impact on people across different levels in the organization leading to potential job losses.

Recent changes in CEO's at both Wipro, IBM or Cognizant are examples of leadership change at the top impacting people at various levels of the organization.

- Age: Age is another big factor that influences our ability to be reemployed in case of a job loss. Most organizations in their lookout to bringdown operational costs, are preferring to employ freshers in place of experienced people. This also is leading to potential job losses and once we have reached above 45 and are faced with job loss, it is increasingly becoming difficult to find another irrespective of our skillsets & experience.

The demands of life have expanded too, adding to the ever-increasing expectations that have to be met consistently. What once used to be known as luxury & comfort have no become necessities. The wants are becoming needs with a great pace. The social networks have also broadened the horizons that impact & influence our needs.

These disruptions & demands of life enhance our anxiety levels to an extent at which it starts impacting our health. There are primarily four aspects of health that we need to look into, assess how we are feeling about each of those, and find ways to course correct or address them right at the onset. The four aspects to look into are:

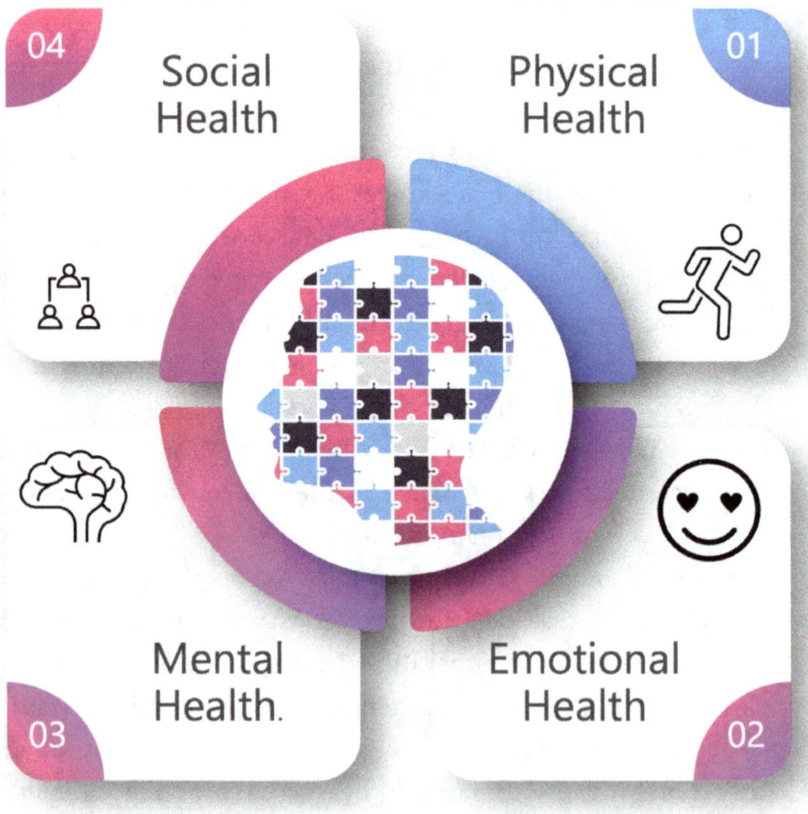

SUDHA CHANDRAN
Indian Film Actress

Sudha Chandran is an Indian actress who appears in Indian films and Television shows. She is an accomplished Bharatanatyam dancer. In May 1981, at about 16 years old, in Tamil Nadu, Sudha met with an accident in which her legs were wounded. She received initial medical treatment of her injuries at a local hospital and was later admitted to Vijaya Hospital at Madras. After doctors discovered that gangrene had formed on her right leg, amputation was required.[10] Chandran says that this period was the toughest time of her life. She subsequently regained some mobility with the help of a prosthetic Jaipur foot. She returned to dancing after a gap of two years and performed in India, Saudi Arabia, United States, UK, Canada, UAE, Qatar, Kuwait, Bahrain, Yemen and Oman .

She started her film career with "Mayuri" which was based on her own life story which was well appreciated by all audience. She went on to bag national award for essaying the role. Her biography is part of curriculum for school children in the age group of 8-11.

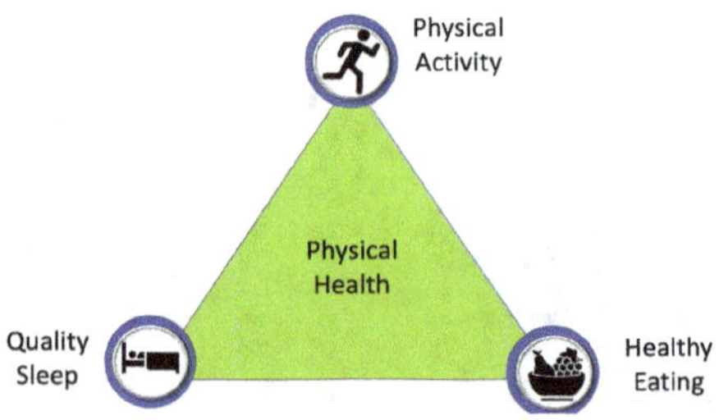

PHYSICAL HEALTH

"A healthy body leads to a healthy mind & vice Versa" - Zig Ziglar

When we refer to physical health, we mostly attribute it to us undertaking physical activity, whether it's doing yoga or running or any other form of physical exercise, that's what we attribute it to. But physical health also involves two other aspects. One is the quality of our sleep, which greatly influences how healthy we are, and also what we eat on a daily basis, because that does contribute to our body and the system, which then influences our other elements of health, whether it is our emotional health or mental health. Since all these are closely coupled, together they influence the social health status of an individual.

Also, when we look at physical health in order to build physical resilience, we need to build physical strength, understand how it affects your overall wellbeing, and how it starts influencing our wellbeing from a mental perspective because we carry the whole stress in our body. When we're physically healthy, which is about being active, eating & sleeping well. That definitely starts positively impacting the way we think, feel, act and how we perceive the world around us.

"Exercise is king & Nutrition is queen, put them together & you have a kingdom" - Jack Lalanne

The second aspect of Physical Health is about healthy eating. It's a well-known fact that if we eat healthy, we feel good about our body. That means we are not carrying any negative influences of what we are eating, which essentially gives us the energy to actually focus on other aspects of health, whether it is our emotional health, or our mental health.

Last but not the least, another significant aspect of physical health that could influence all other elements is the quality of sleep. And we say a good night's sleep. It is very crucial for a healthy mind and a healthy body. And many times, when we are too stressed or when we are facing life is too demanding of us, people even suggest a power nap of even 15 minutes, 30 minutes or an hour, whatever we are used to. And we see that take a great sleep that we had, with absolutely no distractions in our mind or the environment around us, we kind of loose ourself (positively).

This essentially means whatever we have in our mind or whatever emotions we are carrying in our heart are mostly gone by. And when we wake up post that sound sleep, we are as fresh as we would be on any given day when we are completely healthy. That is the significance of physical health. And it's very crucial to focus on, when we are trying to Bounce Back, because it definitely integrates and impacts all other elements or aspects of health, that we are, Or we would be referring to next & onwards.

EMOTIONAL HEALTH

*"It's hard to sleep when your heart is at war with your mind" -
Shayari.com*

Emotional health is the second element of whole health that we have. What does it mean to be emotionally healthy? It's about how we are feeling currently, what is our state of awareness about our emotions? How present we are to our emotions? what is the level of consciousness we have about what we are feeling in general about our life now? how is our workplace environment impacting us? How is our family life impacting us? How is the social environment or the network that we have built is impacting or influencing us? when I say impacting, it could be both positively and negatively. All of these contribute to our emotional health, which is about our feelings, the emotional state. So, when we are going through, or when we're facing disruptions in life due to whatever circumstances we are in, our emotional state defines how we perceive the disruption, and the range of emotions it creates which influences how we think, analyse & act.

Our emotional state defines how we sense, perceive, and process the inputs / information / energy coming both from within ourselves as well as the environment & people around us. These sensations can overtake or cloud our judgement of the reality and coerce us into taking actions which would be detrimental to us, people & environment around us.

Most people are ignorant about their emotional health and operate in an Autopilot mode, reacting to situations unaware of what is driving them to be the persons they are. Those who have the awareness, spend a lot of their energy in suppressing the emotions because they firmly believe the emotions are blocking them from accomplishing their objectives in life.

Lack of focus on Emotional Health either due to lack of awareness or ignorance is detrimental and takes us away from the complete realities of life. We start looking at things, situations & people the way we like to, rather than like what & who in reality they are.

If we focus on either what has already happened, which is negatively impacting our lives at this time, or what we are potentially assuming to happen, or probably would happen based on what is visible to us, how much is visible, and the level of uncertainty that we are facing at this time, it starts building the level of anxiety within our system about that particular uncertainty.

Anxiety about either what has happened in the past or what is going to happen in the future makes us lose out your focus on the present, where we need to respond. It also makes you lose your cognition as well. Our feelings definitely influence our ability to think, what to think about and it then starts impacting what direction we chose, what actions we take? Because when we think wrong, we take wrong actions. When we think right, we will possibly take right actions, we will not always end up getting the right results, but at least we're doing the right things in life that that can bring great results if done consistently. So that is where emotional health comes a lot into picture.

Emotional Health is another integral part to building resilience. If we're able to build a higher level of emotional intelligence, which deals with developing self-awareness, self-management, social awareness and social management, then we are able to have a positive outlook to life or realistic outlook to life to understand where we stand today, and what we can do about the uncertainty that we are facing.

This influences our thought process, which is our third aspect of health, our mental health. If we are emotionally, healthy sound, then we do have a great chance of maintaining our mental health as well. Of course, it is not always, directly relational, but then still there is a sense of balance that we can bring in. If we are emotionally balanced, we can influence your thought process. Even if we are not, at least we are aware of what we are thinking.

So the emotional stability influences the level of awareness, level of consciousness & of course, level of presence. we will have visibility to the thought process and the cognitive intelligence to understand pragmatically, what the reality is? what could be the potential opportunities & threats, because it is not clouded by your emotions.

The next level of attaining Emotional Health is about being emotional agility, a concept coined by Susan David. Emotional Agility helps us overcome the feeling of being stuck, embrace the change, become the disruptors than manage the disruption which results in thriving & excelling bot at work & life.

MAHABHARATA

Mahabharata, an ancient Indian epic, has enlightening verses about a number of, perhaps all, issues that affect our daily lives. It is replete with examples of how damaging negative emotions can be. Anger, one of the negative emotions, is well exemplified and discussed in this epic.

Much earlier in the epic when the princes-the Kauravas and the Pandavas are in their educative years under the tutorship of Dronaachaarya, the Guru gives the pupils assignments. On one such occasion, he enunciates ten principles that he wants the pupils to learn. The next day, when the Guru asks the students what they have learnt, all but Yudhishthira parrot out the enunciated principles. When the latter is asked, he states that he has learnt the first principle, but is not yet thorough with the second. Dronaacharya, less than exemplary himself in the control of anger, is enraged and begins to thrash the eldest Pandava. The prince takes the thrashing in a composed fashion.

Seeing him so composed, Dronaachaarya suddenly realizes that something may be amiss. Pausing, he ponders, "This future King who could get me executed with just one order, is unperturbed by my wrath.... The first principle I taught him was to always be truthful; the second was to control one's temper...!" The teacher immediately realizes his folly and senses the prince's sincerity in truly learning a principle. The guru embraces the prince and compliments him on his sincere learning of two principles, whereupon the Prince responds, "Sir! I haven't really mastered the second at all. But the first I am evincing even now. Just now as you were beating me, my ire was ignited and I have really struggled to keep it under control."

MENTAL HEALTH

"Thoughts could leave scars deeper than almost anything else" - Madam Pomfrey

If we're not really caring about our physical health or our emotional health or both, then we slowly start negatively impacting our mental health as well. And we all know degradation of physical health is more an accepted fact in people around us, even with ourselves, but degradation of emotional health or mental health is still seen as something which is not generally acceptable. People still don't see or accept someone who probably had, or has mental health issues or emotional health issues, treat them as normal human beings and, probably are not generally empathetic towards them. We are still not in that state of maturity as a society and see them as a taboo even today.

We are very guarded against in involving or including people with mental issues in our journey of life. That is something which is clearly visible. So from that point of view, it's very important to focus on the mental health too, which together with our physical & emotional health influences social health.

The three together define who we are and that understanding of who we are, defines How well we can visualize yourself? How we perceive people around us? How the perception influences our current state? how well we can manage ourselves would then influence the way we perceive the world around us. Our perception then starts influencing how we look at life and how much of an impact the social environment within which we are operating or our social network that we are interacting with, can impact you whether positively or negatively.

We get caught in a continuous perception loop and struggle to find a way out. The more we get stuck in this loop, the stronger & deeper the stigma becomes. Without a way out, this can lead to us taking extreme decisions leading to loss of lives or creating an irretrievable damage. Change is the only constant and the disruption that it brings is growing exponentially bringing along equal amount of uncertainty with it.

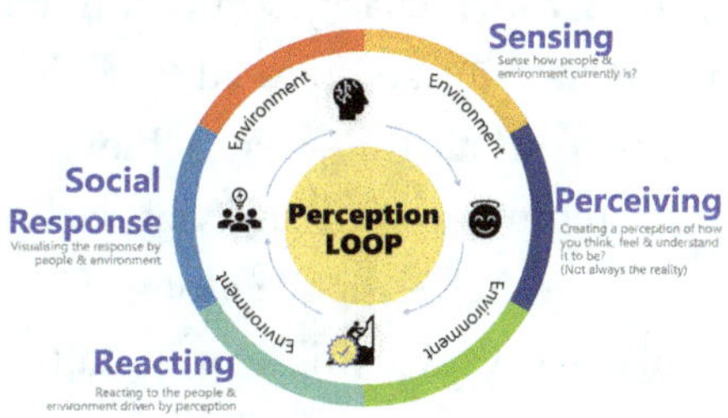

Resilience is the core competence that we need to build & integrate into our personality & character in order for us to navigate through these disruptions and continue to thrive & excel. While resilience alone does not give us all the ammunition needed to win, it will help us to the ability to stand-up and fight. The outcome will then be decided by the other personality traits & actions we devise for ourselves, the grit, determination and the commitment we show in our resolve to win.

"Status Quo, you know is Latin for the mess we are in" - Ronald Regan

This again is not a one-time effort, it is something we need to consistently develop and evolve as the stronger the disruption, the greater the resilience we need.

If we have the right feeling about where we are, have the right way of thinking about what our situation is, then we are able to visualize what strengths we have currently that could help us to address the uncertainty. We may not completely overcome the uncertainty if it's not still visible to us, especially if the event has not occurred, we can prepare ourself to face what's about to hit us because we would have visualized & considered the worst possible impact.

The second scenario is where we are already impacted, then it still gives us a sense of reality, gives you a clear picture of where you stand with reference to the impact the situation has in your context. This creates a level of acceptance which changes our thinking from "Why this happened to me?" to "What we can do to address the situation?" That's what we need to learn from all the great achievers, neither did they succeed at their first attempt nor success was served to them readily on a platter. They all have the resilience along with a combination of other personality traits that they exhibit on a daily basis, to fight the odds stacked against them and never QUIT.

The core to their success was having clarity about what is within their control, and do everything possible to control the controllables. Controlling the controllables comes from having that awareness & visibility of what we can control in a given context. This again is not a one-time effort, it is something we need to consistently develop and evolve. The stronger the disruption, the greater the resilience we need.

In order to Bounce Back, we need to build awareness of three types of objectives that are focused on Growth through disruption, Maintaining current ways of life and Sustenance. The three types of objectives that we can classify are:

- Audacious Objectives - These objectives are still growth oriented and focused on accomplishing next level in our careers or our quality of life.
- Pragmatic Objectives - These are focused on maintaining our current life style and moving into horizontal roles and trying to be more conservative about what we want.
- Sustenance Objectives - These are focused on worst case scenario and focus on what's mandatorily needed for us to survive while we are looking for ways to move at focusing on more pragmatic or growth objectives.

Once we are able to define these three very clearly, we would know where we are currently and how long we can sustain the current way of life, what we need to cut down based on how well we are able to progress up or down the Pyramid of objectives.

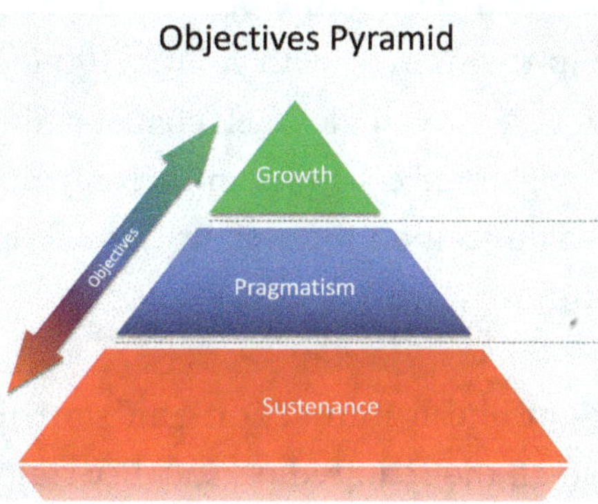

The next section of the book outlines the various personality traits that we need to equip ourselves with in order to successfully navigate through the disruption and be able to Bounce Back.

These personality traits have been identified after carefully studying the lives of various people who have been faced with extreme situations in their lives and have successfully managed to come out winners giving us all required motivation, energy, positivity and belief that we too can Bounce Back if we are able to put our efforts in the right direction.

In Section 3, we will outline a 10 steps framework that will provide a method to use the various personality traits outlined in Section 2 and follow the framework step by step for us to **BOUNCE BACK**, to not just survive but thrive & excel.

Section 4 of the book also includes a self-help workbook which has all the questions that help us look inward, challenge our thought process, mindset, beliefs, behaviours and contextualize the framework to build a roadmap with a set of clear actions.

The last section of the book contains all the templates of various artefacts that are mentioned throughout the book. This enables the reader of this book with the methodology, the framework, the tools & techniques to help themselves with minimal guidance needed from anyone else. However, if you do feel challenged even after going through the complete set of exercises in arriving at what is right for you, we encourage you to look for a right coach whom you can trust and take your journey forward.

Let's jump straight ahead into action and start building & flexing our muscles to build all the required personality traits through Section 2. We are excited, what about you??

"Individually we are a drop, together we are an ocean" - Ryunosuke Satoro

SOCIAL HEALTH

The National Association of Social Workers defines social health as "the quality of an individual's social life, including the level of satisfaction with interpersonal relationships, self-acceptance, and mutual support." Social health is the level of well-being that someone has in their social sphere.

We are all influenced by our social environment, and the way that we interact with others in person, on social media, or through other digital mediums can have a huge impact on our mental health. Physically, an individual's social health affects the way they move through their day-to-day life. Some people might take up smoking habitually to break the ice when meeting new people. Someone who feels lonely might use alcohol as it brings them closer to another human being. Social isolation could lead to depression, while lack of exercise may be linked with hypertension. These are only some examples; there are many more ways that changes in your physical and emotional state can affect your social health and vice versa. The WHO identifies these areas of concern as the determinants of ill-health and states that "social factors contribute significantly to the burden of disease."

The social health of a person is as important as their mental and physical health. The social interactions that we find in our everyday lives can provide us with the necessary components to live a fulfilling life. If you feel like you're struggling with any aspect of your life, connecting to others will help you to improve your situation.

The importance of family: Family is one of the most important interactive components, and it provides many opportunities for social engagement. Whether it's something as simple as chatting over coffee or enjoying a barbecue together, family can be a source of strength and stability for those we cherish most.

Why you should care: People who feel connected to others have better overall health because they are more likely to engage in healthy behaviors such as eating well and exercising regularly. They also tend to experience less stress, which may impact their quality of sleep. This enhances our stability of mind which helps us focus better on situation at hand, focus on reality and look forward in life than being caught in a continuous loop of cause & effect.

Importance of Networking: Networking is an intricate process that requires not only hard work but also the ability to be social. The benefits of networking are numerous, but there are three major benefits that are most noticeable. First, networking can help build a good reputation. Second, it helps form connections up the chain of command. Third, it improves chances for advancement in one's current position. The last benefit is especially important when comparing to other types of job searches. Since networking can be done face-to-face or virtually in the digital environment we are operating in, it gives us the ability to positively influence people even without meeting them. Most jobs today are being filled with candidates through references than directly through marker. This makes networking very crucial since it allows candidates to use the strength of their relationships to make it to a new job or new role in the current organization.

Building a good social network

Technology is an important part of our everyday lives. We use the internet to communicate, connect with friends and family, learn new things, and so on. Today, social media sites like LinkedIn, Facebook, Twitter, and Instagram are the most popular ways to connect with other people. But what does this mean for your social health? It can be hard to tell if you're connecting with people online or getting more isolated. While there are pros and cons to both options, we do know that using these websites has its benefits. For example, collecting information about yourself through pictures, videos, and status updates can provide insight into how others perceive you.

Another great way to improve your social health is to start talking with strangers. By doing so, you'll get out of your comfort zone and meet some new people. Finally, when you work on improving your overall social health, you can also benefit from strengthening your relationships at home, at work and beyond work with the larger community.

How to grow your network:

- **Talk to people about meaningful subjects:** If you want to build your network, don't just surround yourself with people who are the same as you. Instead, talk to people about important things and meaningful subjects to diversify your own thought process, respect their views to broaden your own perspectives. Add value to them and to yourself too.
- **Spend time with people who are good for you:** Social health is important for anyone to maintain healthy relationships and the ability to make friends. Spending time with people who are good for you can be beneficial in many ways. One way is that your mental health will improve and you will feel more satisfied with your social interactions and relationships. Additionally, spending time with supportive people may help you become less stressed, anxious, sad, lonely, depressed, angry, jealous, or worried. Lastly, spending time with positive individuals can motivate you to live a happier lifestyle with more positive outlook to life.
- **Get in the habit of doing something nice for someone else:** Doing something nice for someone else is a great way to spread joy and happiness. It can even be as simple as giving time to someone to be a sounding board to bounce off their situation

or ideas. Though people may think of themselves as selfish, it is important to remember that we all need to take care of our social health and make sure we do something nice for others every day.

- **Keep up your social media habits:** Social Media is a powerful tool that can be used to help people connect with others, increase awareness of different causes, and create different types of jobs. Being consistent with your thoughts and ways you represent yourself; you can build your credibility in your network. The more consistent you are in providing value for people within your domain of expertise, the more influential you start becoming. The intent should be of providing value to everyone you interact with and being grateful for the opportunity.

- **Encourage others:** Many of us have been in a situation where we had to encourage someone else. We all know how hard it can be to provide encouragement and support when we are struggling with our own lives and issues. One of the most powerful ways we can encourage others is by giving them understanding and empathy. When we meet someone for the first time, it is important that we don't judge them on their appearance, lifestyle, or outward persona. Instead, we should try to get inside their head so that we understand what they are going through. Once this connection has formed, then we can truly give support instead of judgment and criticism. By encouraging others, we ourselves will begin to improve and become healthier people.

Five tips for improving your social health:

- **Spend time with friends:** Studies have shown that spending quality time with close relatives promotes happiness. In fact, research has also found that having a healthy relationship with parents predicts longevity. When family members spend quality time together, it strengthens relationships between generations and reduces loneliness. Spending time with friends helps with moods; if we see someone unhappy around us, we give off happy vibes which encourages them to smile too.

- **Talk to Others:** When we talk about ourselves or share an experience with other people, we are able to express our emotions and reduce negative feelings such as anxiety and stress. By sharing experiences with friends and family, they become part of our own personal history and we gain strength from each other.

- **Have good communication skills:** Communication skills are essential when we want to improve our social health. We communicate through words, facial expressions, gestures, and tone of voice. People who demonstrate nonverbal behaviours, such as smiling, laughing, nodding, eye contact and smiling, are more likely to be seen as attractive than people who don't use these positive body language signals.

- **Practice mindfulness:** Mindfulness is the ability to focus on what's happening in present moments without judgment. It can bring us closer to others because we are less concerned with memories or future plans. Instead, we live fully in the moment, accepting whatever happens while being curious about how different events affect us. Finally, empathy, the practice of meditation builds awareness and concentration, allowing the mind to calm down, reducing emotional reactivity and making us happier and healthier (WHO).

Measurement: There are many different ways to measure a person's social health, including: the size and quality of their network, how close they are with others, and various psychosocial scales. Some examples include:

- **Network Size:** How large is your social network? Is it small (less than 5) or large (more than 20)? What percentage of your network would belong to the same type as yourselves? Quality of

Relationship-How well are you connected with people in your network? Do you feel comfortable asking someone else for help, or have difficulty in reaching out to others?

- **Social Support:** Are there people in your network, who will always be available to listen and offer help? Who are those people? Would another person be willing to support you if needed?
- **Psychosocial Health:** Other measures that go beyond general happiness levels and instead look specifically at affective components of mental health. These measures usually take the form of self-report questionnaires. Examples include the following:
    - Perceived Stress Scale – This scale looks at stressors specific to an individual.
    - General Health Questionnaire – The GHQ includes four subscales measuring depressive symptoms, anxiety, somatic complaints, and social dysfunction.
    - Rosenberg Self Esteem Scale – This scale focuses on positive self-esteem and negative feelings about oneself.
    - Center for Epidemiologic Studies Depression Scale – The CESD has 10 questions designed to assess negative moods.

A person's social health has a very close connection to their economic well-being as those with high social health are more likely to be employed and able to work effectively for longer periods of time. Having positive relationships with family members, coworkers, and friends contribute to higher levels of current and future life satisfaction. Social health also contributes to the effectiveness of our immune system. When we interact with others, stress hormones such as cortisol decrease. This decreases the reactivity to new situations or stimuli in the environment, making us less reactive to things that may be threatening. It helps strengthen immunity and makes us healthier overall.

SANDEEP SINGH
Even a bullet couldn't stop him hit his goals

Sandeep Singh (born 27 February 1986) is an Indian professional field hockey player from Haryana and an ex-captain of the Indian national hockey team. He generally featured as a full back and was a penalty corner specialist for the team. He was famous as Flicker Singh in media. Sandeep's international debut was in January 2004 in Sultan Azlan Shah Cup in Kuala Lumpur.

On 22 August 2006, Singh was seriously injured after being hit by an accidental gunshot in the Kalka Shatabdi Express train, while on his way to join the national team due to leave for the World Cup in Africa two days later. He was almost paralyzed and on the wheelchair for 1 year of his life. He was 20 at that time.

Singh not only recovered from that serious injury but also established himself again. Under his captaincy, the Indian team managed to clinch the Sultan Azlan Shah Cup in 2009 after defeating Malaysia in the finals at Ipoh. India won the title after a long wait of 13 years.

The India men's national field hockey team qualified for the 2012 Summer Olympics in London after a gap of 8 years. The team had a resounding victory over France in the finals of the Olympic qualifiers by beating France 9–1. Singh was the highest scorer of the Olympic qualifiers tournament by scoring 16 goals.

2

PERSONALITY TRAITS TO BOUNCE BACK

"We all get distracted, the question is, would you bounce back or bounce backwards?" - Kendrick Lamar

There are numerous stories from history where you have people from diverse backgrounds, professions, businesses, cultures etc facing the most adverse situations in their lives which pushed them down to the dumps. They didn't get bogged down by the situation or impact, instead, they crawled, fought back to accomplish success, set an example for others to look up to and emulate.

If you reflect closely on these stories, you would definitely find certain common personality traits & characteristics they had which helped them overcome the odds and make it to the top. Before we introduce the framework which can provide a path for you to face the disruptions in your own life, fight them and come-out as winners, we need to look at these common traits and understand them well.

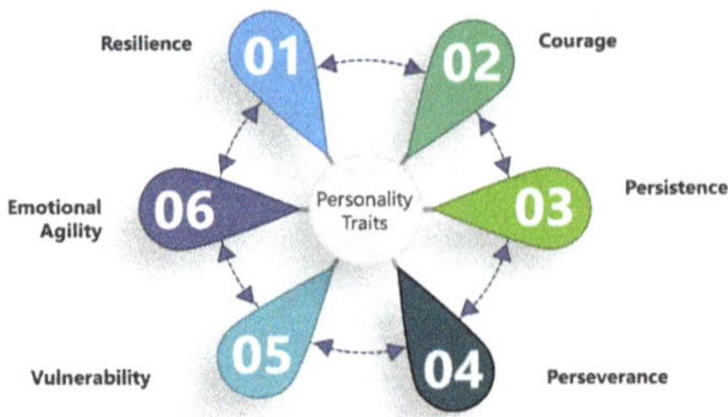

For any framework to be put to good use, you need to introspect who you are, what your belief system is, what personality traits you have built into your system that influences your behaviors & responses to different situations you face in life.

Once you are clear about who you are and what characterises that, you can start looking at what you need to change within yourself to change the way you think, make decision and respond to the situation at hand.

Without the above in place, no framework can really help you. The only person if at all you can attempt to change in order to change the situation is yourself. The below personality traits make it possible for you to progress on that journey of change and accomplish who want to be.

RESILIENCE

Resilience tops the list of most common traits of all the warriors who fought their way out of the adversities and claimed victory. Before we look at other traits, let's dig a bit further into what Resilience is? why it is the most significant trait to build into our personality? and How it helps us to stage a fight against the adversities?

"Resilience is our ability to embrace adversity & uncertainty that comes out of it".

Resilience doesn't guarantee success but it keeps us in the game of life, makes us look at life to be full of possibilities rather than constraints. It gives us the ability to celebrate failures, not ridicule them, drives our focus to what we can learn from their failures instead of harping on why it happened.

Resilience moves us from the past to present and helps us to visualize potential positive future. The optimism that stems out of us being resilient gives us the energy, motivation, drive, grit & determination to continue our journey towards success. The more adversities we face & overcome, the more resilient we become, the more successful we will be.

Mckinsey & Company released in interesting article in early 2021 regarding the frequency of disruption over the past few decades. The data clearly indicates that the disruption is becoming quite frequent and the impact being exponential. The authors rightly say "2020 was a wake-up call for everyone around the world. To thrive in the coming decade, companies must develop resilience - the ability to withstand unpredictable threat or change and then to emerge stronger.

"People Who are resilient people possess three characteristics — They can visualize & accept reality the way it is; strong belief system that life is full of possibilities, and an uncanny ability look at failures as learnings. we can bounce back from any adversity or face any level of disruption if we are resilient enough. "

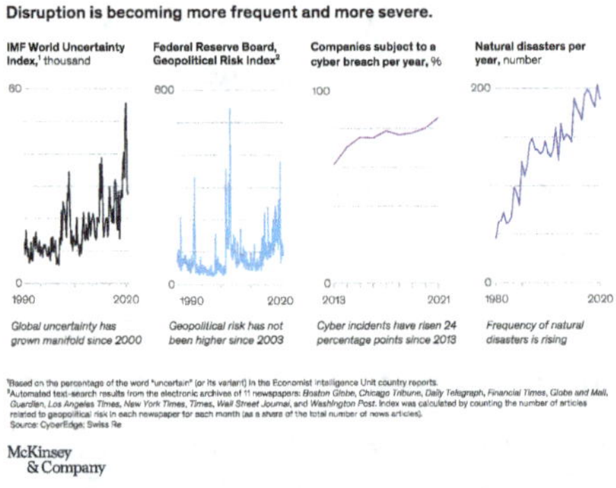

This holds good not just for individuals but also organizations as well. Organizations with resilient leadership inculcate a culture that can face reality with staunchness, make a meaning out of adversity, and continuously innovate / improve to thrive.

How do we build resilience:

- **Change the perspective:** Most of us are prone to look at the negativities & risks of making a decision or taking an action or facing a situation. When we are at cross-roads in life, we always look to take the least resistance path and that is our natural tendency. When faced with uncertainty in life or when life is disrupted, instead of thinking "Why this happened to me?" or "Why am I always the chosen one?", we need to change the way we look at the situation. Start thinking about "How can I address the situation? what opportunities is this situation providing? Presenting ourselves with potential opportunities provides a positive outlook to life. Changing the perspective is about moving from constraints to possibilities.

- **Embrace the situation:** Whenever we are faced with disruption, the first reaction that we exhibit is denial. Our reaction starts with "This can't happen to me". Denying an event that has occurred already doesn't in anyway change it. The sooner we accept the reality the faster we can look for possible ways to overcome the situation. Embracing the situation is about accepting it willingly.

- **Identify your fears:** We all avoid looking inward in order to not come face to face with our utmost fears. This means we most of the time live with a sense of false identity fooling ourselves even though we understand our fears. In order to build resistance, we need to start acknowledging our fears and build strength to face them. We will never reach a stage of being fearless in life and that is not the intent either. It's about our ability to increase our awareness of our fears, acknowledge them and face them with right earnest.

- **Practice Mindfulness:** Mindfulness is a mental state achieved by focusing one's awareness on the present moment, while calmly acknowledging and accepting one's feelings, thoughts, and bodily sensations. It's about our ability to be fully present in the now and focusing on what is happening within us because of the situation we are in. Practicing mindfulness helps us to be visible to our emotions, thoughts, feelings at any given point of time, which means we have accomplished a higher state of conscious-ness & awareness. With awareness comes acknowledgement & acceptance.

- **Believe in your strengths:** At the time of distress caused by disruption, we tend to focus on negatives, our weaknesses in this case. "I can't do this", "I don't have these skills", "I don't know these technologies", "I shouldn't have been in this sector" etc. are the statements that we mostly relate to. However, in order to change the perspective from constraints/limitations to possibilities and create a sense of optimism, we need to shift our focus to our strengths, how we have used them so far, and our strong beliefs, values that helped us accomplish success so far in our career.

  Revive all our old memories to identify our strengths that we have relied on, talk to people whom you trust and get a feed-back on what all they noticed as your strengths over the period that you have engaged with them. These could help us build optimism for our future.

- **Define possibilities:** Knowing our strengths & limitations is the key to defining possibilities for building a sustainable future. Based on our strengths, we define what opportunities they high-light, how those strengths serve us to choose, create a positive environment and help you bounce back.

  Look at what skills & competencies we can make use of, are there any that we can learn & adapt to driven by our strengths that can reveal a larger set of opportunities.

  Review our personal & professional network, level of influence we have, strength of our relationship & trust with each of them and their level of influence within their networks as well. This analysis will help us in more than one way:
  - Understand whom we can reach out, to validate what we have identified as opportunities and seek their inputs on any additional opportunities they visualise for us.

- ○ Seek emotional support from them, reinforce our strengths and enhance our sense of positivity & optimism
  - ○ Understand where they can help us, where we can seek support from them to make the best of opportunities that we have identified.

COURAGE

"Courage is the ability to manage & overcome our fears in the face of adversity and disruption".

Courage is a complimentary to resilience. Courage comes from clarity about the adversity or disruption, it's probability of occurrence, the potential threats & possibilities etc. Without clarity & level of certainty about uncertainty, we would keep crying in despair without hope & optimism. It's not absence of fear, it's the ability to stand tall and face fear with confidence.

"All our dreams come true if we have the courage to pursue them" - Walt Disney

Embracing courage gives us the ability to change our perspective from being pessimistic to being optimistic or moving from despair to hope. It also helps us to face failures, look at what we can learn from them and what we can do differently going forward.

How do we boost our courage?

- **Acknowledge your fears:** Courage is not lack of fears. It's actually about being aware of, acknowledging & accepting our fears. Fear is designed to protect us. It is intended to show us where we can fail and keep us away from it. But lack of awareness or acknowledgement can make It stop us from doing the things we should or could be doing. Fear if not acknowledged and managed, can make us swing to either of two extremes, being too defensive or aggressive, causing us to be too conservative or careless. There are many failures that we would fear, like:
  - Fear of being hurt
  - Fear of missing out
  - Fear of rejection
  - Fear of losing our relations
  - Fear of social backlash
  - Fear of scrutiny
  - Fear of Law
  - Fear of judgement and many more

However, when used positively, It can push us towards our growth and keep our efforts in check fully understanding our strengths & limitations. It highlights the boundaries we currently have around ourselves and then it is up to us to workout how much & how quickly we want to extend our horizons.

Fears drive us either to focus too much into our past (What has gone wrong) or into our future (What could go wrong). It takes completely away from the present reality of life which should be our primary driver.

Few ways to manage our fears is:

- **List down all our fears:** Listing down all our fears can help us know ourselves a lot better, it highlights what matters most to us, what our beliefs are, what our limitations are, what we value etc. Until unless we realise these, it is impossible to manage our fears. Once we list down our fears, start listing positive outcomes we can achieve by going beyond those fears. These are the motivators we can use to manage those fears more effectively.

For ex: One of the most popular fears is Fear of Public Speaking. The possible negative outcomes we focus on, for us to fear about public speaking could be:

- Being an imposter
- Being looked at as a novice on the topic
- Being criticised for our views
  Now if we shift our focus to positive outcomes that could emerge from public speaking:
- We can present our unique perspectives of the topic which will be liked.
- We can share our personal experiences which add great value to people listening
- We can increase our brand value by speaking on topics that we have great expertise & experience on.

Looking at alternate outcomes which show us the benefits of managing our fears can motivate us to take actions required and extend our horizons.

- **List out your excuses:** Self-doubt is a natural emotion and the first to creep in as soon as we are faced with disruption. For some, it makes them slow down their pace and for others, it may make them completely stop from reacting or responding to the situation.

  Excuses most likely are going to make them feel better about not taking action and hold them back from taking much needed actions to bounce back. Excuses make us rationalise our inaction. Look at the list of fears we have outlined and positive outcomes that we have listed if we are able to manage those fears. Now list down the all excuses that we are making for ourselves, for each of the opportunities listed which could drive positive outcomes.

The best way to build our courage to face fears is to stop making excuses for our inaction. Once done, we can look for our motivators that will help us build momentum and keep us on track to bounce back.

- **Define cost of inaction:** For each of the opportunities & the excuses listed, think about what we are losing due to inaction (not acting on the possibilities). The focus should be on quantifying the impact, whether it could be financial, relational, reputational etc. The cost of inaction should be compelling enough to force us into acting on those possibilities.

  All three aspects listed so far above give us a complete clarity about what our perspective is, how to change it, what are our fears that can stop us, what excuses are we justifying ourselves with and what is the impact of our inaction. These should be good enough to challenge our beliefs, drive and motivate us into taking actions.

- **Engage in small acts of bravery:** However, we still need a starting point and it's always advisable to start small. If we are habituated to be fearful about starting anything new, it doesn't make sense for us to start with something big right at the outset.

From the list of possibilities, identify the one we are most comfortable starting off with. This can help us start off from the block and look ahead towards bouncing back.

- **Celebrate your courage:** Once we are able to get off the block and take action. Don't worry too much about the outcomes, the outcomes will happen over due course of time. Celebrate our actions. Celebrate us making the first move off the block, let all our significant supporters know. This gives us great positive reinforcement to evolve and take bigger leaps ahead.

- **Take a bigger leap:** Now that we have staved off the starting problems and taken the first steps, start taking up on the next set of opportunities. Identify actions, stakeholders & support groups who can guide, collaborate, inspire us to progress on those opportunities ahead.

Start reflecting on what positive outcomes we have accomplished through every step of building our courage and how it is serving us to bounce back. Celebrate every step in our journey with our friends, family, our supporters and our extended network. Spread your positivity like fire and we can see the we receive the same or more amount of positive energy back.

"What we give is what we get". If we want positivity in life, we should start giving out positivity to everyone we interact with.

PERSISTENCE

Persistence has multiple meanings & definitions. In this context,

"Persistence is our ability to consistently follow a defined path till we succeed".

Persistence is driven by our grit, it stops us from giving up and helps us build our endurance in life. The focus is on sticking to a routine which we believe will help us succeed. Persistence is about sticking to the plan by finding ways to overcome all the obstacles we face externally & resistance internally.

"A river cuts through the rocks not because of its power but because of its persistence" - Jim Watkins

It takes high level of self-motivation to do it alone, that is why at least when we are trying to something new, it is always recommended to find a group with similar interest and be part. Thereby it helps us to maintain & enhance our motivation levels when we are low or being overpowered by our resistances.

What helps us develop Persistence?

- **Define Objectives (SMART):** Define objectives that are Specific, Measurable, Achievable, Realistic & Time-bound. Lack of clarity of our purpose, vision & objectives can make us wander in the open world. We need concrete objectives for us to focus. Until unless we are clear about where we want to get to, it is difficult to make a start and steer along a path. It would be like us running in an open field without knowing when & where to stop.

  The SMARTer the objectives, the clearer our path and the more persistent we become towards accomplishing them.

- **Identify Motivators:** Now that we have the objectives clearly identified, let's look at what is driving us to accomplish these objectives? What can keep us motivated to pursue & persist with these objectives through to accomplishment. Identifying "why we want to achieve what we want" is the key factor which can help us to persist with our efforts. Without strong motivators, we will tend to drop off these in between or look for the excuses that we can make for not pursuing them beyond a point.

- **Determine Actions needed:** Like we need our objectives to be SMARTer, our actions which layout our path to accomplishing those should also be SMARTer. For each of the objectives that we have identified, determine concrete action plan along with key results that will help us validate our progress. These actions should be served by our strengths, values & beliefs. We need to also define what success means for each of those objectives? how we measure our success? what support we need for us to stay on course? how we will celebrate our success?

Success need not always be aligned to the final objective that we want to accomplish. We can breakdown the long term objectives to one or more short term objectives that will give us opportunity to celebrate and rejuvenate ourselves with fresh & renewed energy to persist our pursuance of long term objective.

For ex: If becoming a TED Speaker is our objective, we cannot think from Day 1 about it. Assuming we are starting off (May 21 at the time of writing) with our public speaking with no prior exposure or experience, our short term objectives could be:

- Speak at a Meet-up by 31 Jul 21
- Speak at a Local Conference by 31 Oct 21
- Speak at a Regional / Global Conference by 31 Jan 22
- Speak at a TEDx Event by 31 Mar 22
- Speak at 3 TEDx Events by 31 Jul 22
- Speak at TED Event by 31 Oct 2

As we can see, the duration of our journey to accomplishing an objective is defined by the complexity & preparation needed for it. But if we don't define the short-term objectives which keep us motivated consistently, it is difficult to persist. Persistence comes from clear action plan and definition of short-term objectives.

- **Find Partners:** When we are starting something new that we have never done before or something that we feel is hard for us to accomplish or even otherwise, the best way to persist with pursuing it is to get into a group with similar objectives. If we can't find someone aligned with our long term objectives, then it could be even towards short term ones. We are all humans and we all will have our ups & downs it's easy for us to lose track of our objectives and start making excuses to let them go. This is where we need partners who can challenge, push, inspire & sometimes compel us to continue to persist. We may also get motivated or get our competitive spirit up & running when we someone else in the group accomplishing their own objectives.

Being part of a group keeps us in check, creates a sense of social accountability which can be a positive driver for us to persist with our actions.

- **Develop Discipline:** Like many other words, Discipline too has many definitions. In the context of "Developing Persistence", Discipline is "being punctual, focused, encouraged & sticking" to the action plan that we have defined for ourselves day-in day-out.

  Self-Discipline is like our muscles, the more we work on it the more stronger it becomes. It is the ability to stay focused, motivated, pushing ourselves into action irrespective of how we feel, physically, mentally or emotionally. It's about showing up consistently to pursue what we intentionally choose, and do it despite distractions or odds stacked against us.

- **Form Habits:** What we can accomplish is influenced a lot by our habits. We exhibits habits that are unconscious, sub-conscious and conscious. For new habit to be formed, we need to be very aware of our existing habits that need to be unlearned or let go.

  As per Charles Duhigg in his book "Power of Habit" talks about a process in which the brain converts a sequence of actions into an automatic routine, known as "Chunking" and it's the root of how habits are formed.

  Habits emerge because the brain is constantly looking for ways to be more efficient by conserving effort and making every routine into a habit. some habits we are conscious about, some sub-conscious and some are so ingrained into us that we don't even realise those, the unconscious.

  This process of turning routine into a habit, is a three step loop. A Cue, Routine and a Reward.

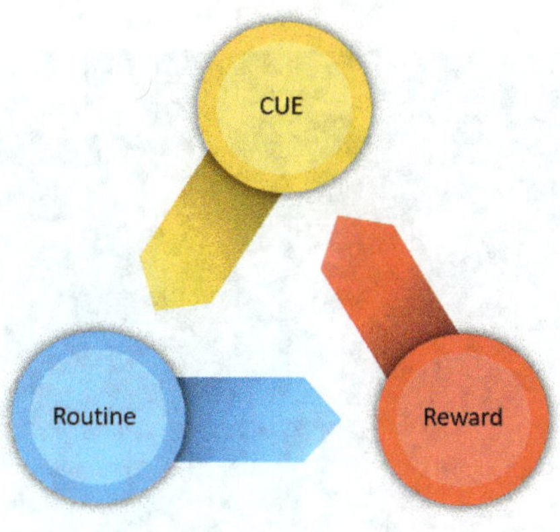

- Cue: A trigger that tells our brain to go into automatic mode and which habit to use.
- Routine: A defined response which can be physical, mental or emotional
- Reward: The final outcome which signals our brain if the habit is worth remembering for the future.

Over a period of time, this loop becomes more & more automatic and the cue & reward become integrated that a great sense of craving for the reward starts emerging and a powerful habit is formed. If we want to change a habit, we need to identify the trigger (primary reason) & the reward (what we crave for) and then change the routine within the habit loop to replace the existing one. Over a period of time, the habit gets changed. The key is to not disturb the complete loop.

Persistence is one of the important traits needed for us to successfully bounce back.

HOW PERSISTENT ARE YOU?

PERSEVERANCE

Persistence alone does not guarantee success. For ex: If we are planning to run a marathon, continuing to just run one or two hours every day in the same terrain, eating same food, following the same routine is not going to help us accomplish our goal. We need a lot of other aspects like our diet, how you time your run, the terrain etc for us to build our core strength along with endurance needed. This is where Perseverance comes into play.

"Perseverance is not a long race, it's many short races one after the other" - *Walter Elliot*

Perseverance is about the flexibility that we bring in while you persist in our pursuit to accomplish what we want to achieve.

For ex: If building a great body is our goal, going to the gym every

day and undergoing the same set of routine builds our endurance but doesn't build a great body. We need to mix & match strength exercises, with weights, targeted muscle building, tightening your abs etc.
If we look at the above example, going to gym everyday defines persistence, bringing variance within what we do while we are at the gym is perseverance.

In our journey to navigate disruption and bounce back successfully, we need both persistence & perseverance in order for us to succeed. They together build grit & determination to continue despite the obstacles we face.

How to develop Perseverance?

- **Overcome fear of failure:** We have already discussed quite a bit about managing our fears in the earlier sections (see "Courage"). However, here we will specifically refer to overcoming "Fear of Failure". This is accomplished by identifying the most compelling reason for us to be successful which serves as our primary driver & motivator to persist.

Continuing with my story of searching for a corporate job: I was looking to get into the corporate world after serving more than two decades in Indian Armed Forces. I was like a frog in the well, fully operating within the confines of our establishment not aware of corporate procedures on hiring, how they would look at Service Veterans, what level of preparation is needed etc.

The good part was that I had started interacting with people from corporate giants like CISCO, HCL, TESCO, WIPRO etc as part of managing a Digital Communications transformation program which gave me a small network of people to start with. But still I didn't have any clue of anything else. I started looking for a job as an IT

Infrastructure Project Manager as I had good background of setting up a communication network from ground up.

This was more than a decade ago and the corporate companies were still not matured enough in understanding the value veterans can bring in. The scenario has changed quite a bit today and there are specific forums driven by diversity to give more opportunities for the veterans. The situation was quite different then and there was no precedence to latch on to.

As I started applying for the Project Manager role, I realised over a period of time that my resume was not passing through their systems as I was not receiving any calls. So I switched my focus on to Walk-In Interviews. I still remember my first interview experience as fresh as it was then. The first call I received was for a Walk-In with IBM and I was required to attend it at DLF IT Park located in Domlur, Bangalore. That was the first instance I was entering an IT park in my life leave alone attending an interview. I spent almost half hour within the parking lot fearing a lot of things, Is my dress code right? How would people react if they know where I am coming from? How to interact with people around me? What are the general etiquettes followed? It was completely an unknown entity and an entirely contrasting environment I was getting into. Lots of apprehensions in my mind running at that time.

Many times during that half hour, the thought of going back did occur. But then, the one thing I fell back to was why I am here? what is driving me? what is that I am looking to accomplish? What purpose this interview serves me? Once I had these questions answered, the compelling need to succeed overtook all the fears & apprehensions I had and went into the interview hall where everyone was seated. I didn't succeed in getting a job out of that interview but if I had returned home that day, I am quite certain that I would never ever again entered an IT Park. (Story continues).

The fact of the matter is if we have to accomplish our objectives, we must have to overcome the fear of failure.

- **Define Resistances:** What we can accomplish is defined by our limitations more than our strengths. Our limitations make us resist taking actions that we know are needed but won't initiate. It's therefore important to list out our resistances that are stopping us from taking the much needed actions and restraining our progress. Only when we are able to visualize, we will be able to overcome. "Awareness leads to action", of course through acknowledgement and acceptance.
Few examples of the resistances I was experiencing were:
- I can't talk to new people
- I can only seek help if I know someone personally
- This particular company is not suitable for me
- I need to fit 100% of the JD for me to apply for the job
These resistances meant that I was losing out on developing relationships, expanding my network, leveraging on people I know and make use of opportunities in front of me.
All that the resistances can do is limit our ability to act on the opportunities visible right in front of us.
- **Build support network:** Most jobs today are visible much earlier in the informal network than on the formal portals whether it is internally within an organization or externally on mediums like LinkedIn or Shine or any other job portals. Having a well-connected network is key to getting your next opportunity in your current organization or in a new one. What we also witness is that people start building their network or even their visibility & brand on social networks only when they are either looking for a change or when they are impacted by layoffs. Establishing a connect or building a good network where we are valued for our contribution to the community which results in increasing our brand value needs consistent effort throughout

our lives. The continuous & consistent sharing of knowledge, experiences and expertise authentically for the community is must for building a strong personal brand. This can be done by the way in which we are able to communicate, by publishing blogs, videos, stories, sharing documents, position papers, speaking at various events, panel discussion, volunteering as reviewers, facilitators, moderators, coaches, mentors & more. There are many people who have apprehensions about making their presence felt on social media. We need to understand that doing what people do on social media comes naturally to only few. Rest all are trying to overcome their fears & apprehensions in their own way. It's important for us to join the bandwagon, understand our constraints, limitations & resistances, look for people whom we can get inspired from, who can support us, challenge us constructively, motivate or coach or mentor us in order to overcome the excuses we are hiding ourselves behind.

I joined LinkedIn on 09 Jan 2010 (that's when I first heard of it) and have grown my network consciously over a period of 11+ years. It has been one of the significant elements to my growth both personally & professionally. I have been using LinkedIn not just to grow my network but also to fast track my progression into a new domain.

Whenever I have to move to a new domain, I look up to the most influencing personalities in that domain on the network and look to connect or follow them. This gives me a good understanding and visibility of what events they follow, the thought leadership they provide, the concepts they refer to, the people they interact with. This definitely speeded up my transition to new domain as against going through traditional learning methods only.

The network once well-established through regular interactions also helps in getting visibility to the jobs much earlier than when they are posted. Another aspect the network can help with is the reference.

There is a lot more weightage & credibility added to our candidature when referred for a job by someone within an organization as against applying it on our own.

So, if you have not yet started building your network or not established your network yet, then the time for action is NOW.

- Set smaller milestones: When we are desperate after job loss or looking at a potential job loss, most of the time we are looking for something big to come our way. There is a sense of urgency though. Instead of looking for a big accomplishment, what we need is to take a step back and set smaller milestones for us to look at accomplishing, that can keep our motivation levels & spirits higher.

Continuing with my story, as I came out of my first interview with IBM, the feedback I got was that they could have progressed my candidature further if I had PMP certification since I was looking for a Project Manager role. That then triggered my next objective, which was to achieve the certification. I then started focusing my efforts towards this objective, registered for a bootcamp, bought Rita Mulcahy's book etc.

When we are looking for a job or any other opportunity to make good for our living, we need to look at breaking down the larger objectives into smaller chunks which we can act on and accomplish in shorter time frame.

- Validate your progress: Once we have established smaller targets to accomplish, we should start taking actions that are required. It's equally important to constantly validate the path we are progressing on, review the lessons learned, how we have evolved through the journey and take the next steps.

Answering below questions during our reflection will help us be better in our next attempt.

- What has gone well during the journey to accomplishing the objective? (that we should continue)
- What has gone well during the journey to accomplishing the objective? (that we should not continue)
- What has not gone well during the journey to accomplishing the objective? (that we should modify/change)
- What has not gone well during the journey to accomplishing the objective? (that we should stop)
- What is that we could have done but didn't (that we should look to start)

Answering all these questions, will help up understand the various aspects that we need to Start, continue, change & stop for us to progress further.

This exercise of review and reflection should be undertaken irrespective of us either being successful or not in accomplishing our short term objective.

Remember, it's not about whether we have been successful or not but it's about how far we have evolved. This focus on continuous evolution takes away our fear of failures and we start looking at failure as a way of learning and evolution. This change in our belief system drives us to try different ways and means to accomplish what we are looking for than getting bogged down after one failure.

- Make the next change: Now that we are getting a hang of making small changes and learning from that, we continue to make changes and take actions towards accomplishing our next shorter objectives while validating our progress towards our long term objective.

Continuing with my story, every time I came out of an interview after I got rejected, my only focus used to be:

- Reflect back on the questions that were asked, how did I respond to them, what were the questions I struggled with or didn't have an answer to etc.

- Another point of reflection also was on, how well I understood the interviewer, how well was I able to engage with them during the conversation, what were their expectations when they asked the questions they did etc.

- And then, redo the interview myself and answer the questions with the renewed understanding which made me ready to express myself better in the next one.

- The ultimate focus then was on how, when and where I could land my next interview.

VULNERABILITY

Vulnerability means many things to many people and there are quite a few definitions around it. Vulnerability in the context of "Bounce Back" is:

Being authentic to self: Authenticity stems from the understanding & awareness of who we are. It also comes from knowing what we fear, how we manage fear, from the ability to visualize our thoughts, emotions, feelings and not judge ourselves on them. Being Authentic is about being real and not being an Imposter. We all are imposters in certain areas of our life, some more and some less. The less we carry the imposter syndrome, the more authentic we are.

Impostor syndrome (also known as impostor phenomenon, impostorism, fraud syndrome or the impostor experience) is a psychological pattern in which an individual doubts their skills, talents, or accomplishments and has a persistent internalized fear of being exposed as an "impostor" - Wikipedia.

While imposter syndrome is mostly associated with us exhibiting it to people around us, what we are referring to here, is exhibiting it to ourselves. The major aspect that influences us to be imposters is level of self-acceptance. Imposter syndrome significantly influences our understanding and realization of our potential due to lack of self-belief.

- **Being open to accept the reality:** Many a time we probably know ourselves well enough but are afraid to accept that reality. This also impacts how we look at the world around us and how much we accept to the reality. Accepting reality, whether it's about ourselves or about the situation we are in or the people around us needs us to overcome being judgemental. It's about always wanting to see, hear, speak only good things about ourselves. We like to acknowledge ourselves for all good things, the successes, the accomplishments because they bring in positivity and the feel good factor. To accept reality, we need to move away from judgement, whether it's good or bad, just acknowledge "it is what it is".

- **Being open enough to acknowledge our failures:** "Failures are steppingstones for success". We all have heard of this phrase numerous time right from our childhood days and probably will keep hearing till our last breath. How we deal with our failures defines how successful we can become.

  Fear of failure is one of the important things to overcome if we want enhance our levels of success. How can we do that? It is by celebrating our failures. Celebrating doesn't mean bursting crackers or cutting cake etc. Celebrating failures means talking about it openly in front of others. Many a times, speaking to others clears lot of things for ourselves, where we went wrong, what we can learn from that, what we could have done differently etc. Lot of reflection comes through when we speak about your failures. That is celebration of failures because we shift our focus from why we failed to what we learn from it and how we could be better.

- **Being empathetic to self:** Even those who practice being empathetic, mostly associate empathy to be external oriented which means we need to empathise with people we are dealing with. But when it comes to ourselves, we are either crucifying, ridiculing, or punishing ourselves most of the times. What we need to practice is Self-Empathy too.

  Remember the routine announcement by cabin crew before a flight takes off, "Pls put on your oxygen mask before you help others". Empathising with self is as important or I would even say more important than empathising with others.

What is Empathy?

As per Karla McLaren, Empathy is a social and emotional skill that helps us feel and understand the emotions, circumstances, intentions, thoughts and needs of others, such that we can offer sensitive, perceptive, and appropriate communication & support.

An empathetic person is someone who can read our emotions, nuances of our behaviors, the intent behind our thoughts and interactions, our body language, energy levels and gestures much easier than many. To be empathetic, we need to understand "Transference & Counter-transference".

Transference: involves establishing an emotional connect with the person you are conversing with, understanding their feelings & emotions, able to integrate into our own system and feel the same within ourselves.

Counter-transference: Involves putting yourself in their situation, understand what they need and being able reflect back a genuine response which sometimes may not be even your own best interests. The genuineness of your response would depend on how well you are able to identify the emotions, thoughts, feelings and intentions of the people you are dealing with, understand your own emotional reaction to those and regulate your own.

How do we practice Self-Empathy?

- **Self-Awareness:** Consistently develop your state of awareness through practice of developing deep consciousness by being present to yourself, listening to your thoughts, emotions, perceptions, biases etc.
- **Self-Reflection:** We all have the ability and do reflect on our actions, feeling, thoughts, emotions etc. However, what is different is at what duration we look to reflect and provide a feedback for ourselves. Hence, what needs to change is the frequency of that reflection & feedback. The faster the feedback loop, the faster we are able to visualize our emotional and mental state which is crucial for developing self-empathy
- **Self-Compassion:** It's the desire to help ourselves to be the best version. Only when we have compassion that we will be able to empathise on what we see through reflection. Without compassion, only awareness & reflection can lead us to a state where we can instil damage to ourselves and people around us.

Tools & Techniques that can be used to develop Self-Empathy: There are many to develop Self-Empathy, few that can be practiced are:

- **Journaling:** This is a tool widely used. Writing down about how your day went, at the end of a day. What emotions, thoughts, feelings you observed? How those served you in dealing with the circumstances? How you can help yourself to be better served when you experience similar thoughts, emotions feelings etc.

- **Empty-Chair:** This is a technique used in Neuro-Linguistic Programming (NLP). Place an empty chair in front of you and visualize yourself to be sitting in that chair. Now express all your feelings, emotions, thoughts to the "other you" sitting in the chair. This helps you to detach yourself from the emotional / mental state and helps you to take a second person view of your state. With certain amount of practice, you will be able to develop a more deeper understanding of yourself, what drives you to behave the way you do and how you can help yourself.

Being open to move out of our comfort zone: It's in human nature to seek comfort in whatever we do and also in the way we lead our life. But it is a well-known fact that "Growth happens only outside of our comfort zone".

Our comfort zone is an emotional space where we sense happiness in our lives, predictability of our lifestyle with minimal risk, stress & anxiety with a routine set of behaviors & actions. There is minimal change to the way we lead our life.

Question is, how do we learn to move out of our this comfort zone?

- **Reflect on past experience:** We all would have at some point in life moved out of comfort zone and tried new things in life. We would have succeeded in some and have learned from some experiences. For ex: Moving from one town to another or one school to another, tried learning a new language, attending first interview, expressing love interest etc. Start reflecting on those situations, understand what drove you to take those steps? This reflection highlights our motivators which drive us out of our comfort zone and also the way we convince ourselves to make our move.

- **Start making small changes:** On daily basis which helps you break your routine and consistently reflect on the experience you achieve from those changes without judgement to categorise them (good or bad).
- **Identify Patterns:** Identify your thought patterns that help you break your routine from time to time and how you can replicate the similar patterns to any given situation which can help you to make that switch to move out of comfort zone.
- **Evolve your change:** Once you understand and are aware of your mental model, you can look to evolve your change to a level that can help you to seek bigger challenges that help you grow personally & professionally.

Being open to seek help: Seeking help is generally considered to be a display of weakness which is absolutely wrong. on the contrary, seeking help is a display of strength, the strength to accept that we are humans and we do have deficiencies, strength of our state of awareness, and strength of our level of consciousness about our emotional or mental state.

- The biggest factor that can stop us from seeking help is our "EGO". It's about the feeling of I can manage myself and we only resort to seeking help only when we reach a state of desperation not earlier.
- Another factor that can stop us is fear of social stigma, How would people feel? How would people respond? How would they treat me? Will my status go down in their eyes? The superior complex that fulfils our ego pulls us away from asking for help.
- Last but not the least, is the trust factor. How much we trust the person whom we want to seek help from? What is the strength of our relationship? How confident we are about their ability to help?

Again all the steps mentioned above for moving out of comfort zone are applicable here too. Reflect on past experiences of asking for help, start with small requests, identify your mental model and validate the level of trust & strength of relationship with people whom you are seeking help and then evolve.

EMOTIONAL AGILITY

"Emotional Agility isn't about whether you are right or wrong, It's about whether your behaviour is serving you" - Susan David

Emotional Agility:

"Emotional Agility is about being flexible with our thoughts and feelings so that you can respond optimally to everyday situations". This is the key to our well-being & success. - Susan David. Emotional Agility is about being aware of our emotions driven by our thoughts, feelings and inferences of the circumstances in and around us. It's also about choosing how to respond to those emotions.

In her book "Emotional Agility", Susan David quotes Viktor Frankl writing "Between stimulus and response, there is a space". In that space is our power to choose our response and in our response lies our growth and our freedom". The more we are aware and able to open that space to reflect on how we feel, what is causing us feel the way we do, gives us the ability to make a better choice of our responses. Without emotionally being agile, more often than not our reactions & choices are driven by how we perceive people around us than the situation itself and how we are actually feeling about the situation & why?

People who are emotionally agile demonstrate a greater sense of self-awareness, self-reflection, self-management leading to better social-awareness and social management. This is absolutely necessary for us to be better at if we are looking to manage disruptions & adversities effectively and thrive. This doesn't mean they are devoid of frustration, feeling lost, angry or despair but they are able to display faster acceptance, self-empathy and curiousness that helps them face the adversities.

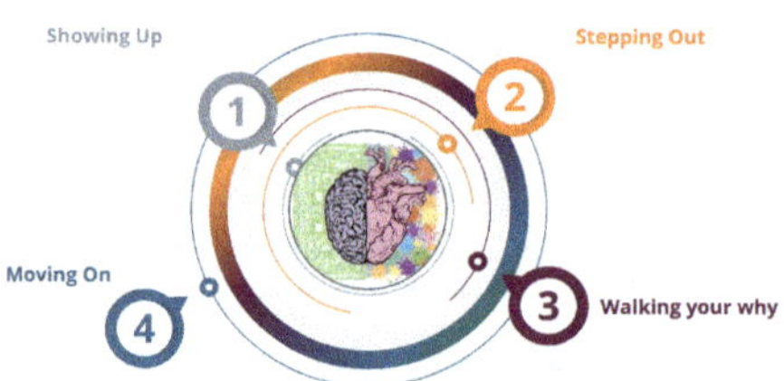

Below are the four steps to accomplish Emotional Agility:

- Showing-up: Facing into your thoughts, emotions & behaviours willingly with curiosity and kindness. We need to cultivate Courage, Self-acceptance & Perseverance to show-up for ourselves everyday & in every situation. It's not always that we will like to see the person visible within us but irrespective, we need to continue to do so.
- Stepping out: Detaching from and observing ourselves for what we are – just thoughts, just emotions, to create non-judgemental space. Usually, "We define ourself based on what we identify ourselves with". To develop emotional agility, we need to learn

to let go of our attachment which pushes us to be judgemental. Judging ourselves based on what we see & observe makes the acceptance harder and clouds our reflection. Self-Empathy and compassion helps us to overcome the natural inclination to be judgemental as they move us from the observations making us define who we are, to why we are the way we are. This is a big shift that is needed for us to start looking at what we can do about it. If we are stuck at "Who we are?" state then we start blaming circumstances & people for our state instead of looking internally and understand the "WHY".

- Walking you why: Recognizing, accepting and then distancing ourselves from our thoughts & emotions gives us the ability to integrate thinking and feeling with long-term aspirations and find new ways of getting there. What is our purpose in life? This needs to be clearly identified & well defined based on our values & beliefs. Once this is clear, we can align all our objectives to our purpose which then can guide our priorities and actions in life.
- Moving on: This is about getting unstuck, there could many ways in which we move on with our lives. A few mentioned below:
  - Tiny Tweaks Principle – Small, deliberate tweaks infused into our routine and habitual parts of life can afford tremendous leverage for change. Identify.
  - The See-Saw Principle - Finding the balance between challenge and competence, so we're neither complacent nor overwhelmed but excited, enthusiastic and invigorated by challenges.

The ultimate goal of Emotional Agility is to keep a sense of challenge & growth alive and balance them well throughout our lives.

3

BOUNCE BACK FRAMEWORK

Bounce Back Framework introduces you to 10 steps that are needed to be undertaken for you to build the right personality traits as well as actions needed to face adversities and overcome disruptions.

Bounce Back Framework

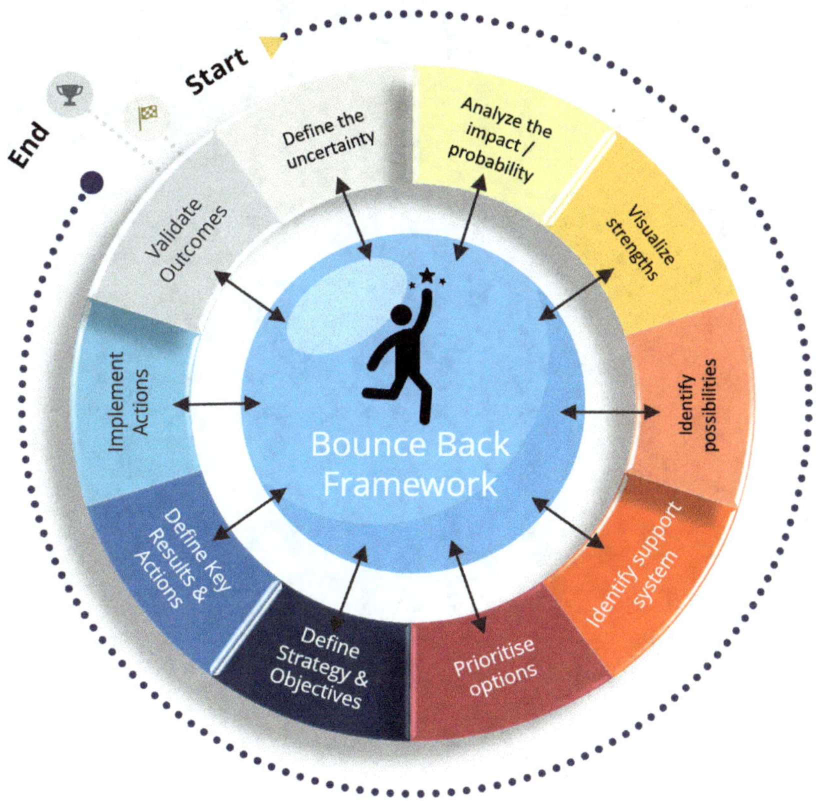

1

Steps 1 - 5

STEP 1: BEING CERTAIN ABOUT UNCERTAINTY

We all love predictability in life but unfortunately life is full of surprises, some we feel manageable and some much difficult. It's not the uncertainty that makes the difference, it's the level of uncertainty the influences how we think & feel about it.

"When nothing is sure, everything is possible"

- Margaret Drabble

"Uncertainty is lack of surety & predictability of future way of life".

The level of uncertainty is driven by the complexity it brings in, the potential impact, prior experience of handling something similar and where we are currently in life. It's the level of uncertainty that drives our comfort levels. The dependencies which could be financial, social, or state of a relationship and the risk appetite we have is defined by the what we are looking for and where we find comfort. It's the fear of unknown that creates anxiety and higher anxiousness leads to desperation.

In order to effectively manage uncertainty, we need to look at bringing down the level of uncertainty to what we are comfortable with. Try to bring clarity about the situation and breakdown the situation further into smaller chunks of events. Align them with the probability of occurrence.

Quoting from my own personal experience a while back:

I am a strong believer in becoming dispensable in my role whichever organization I have been with. That comes from my continuous lookout for new challenges as I am easily bored by standard routine. For me to be able to move into a different domain or different industry sector, it's important that I build sustenance in the current role.

I brought in a new person from within the organization to take up my role and transitioned the responsibilities over a defined period. Once the transition was complete, I started looking for alternate possibilities for myself within the organization. The expectation was that I will be able to find something new that challenges me quite easily with my experience. My performance had been quite good too and I had been recently promoted as well which gave me that confidence.

However, surprisingly there were very few that came my way and I was rejected for those roles post a few rounds of interviews. The future was completely uncertain. Lots of thoughts started floating around, Will I get an opportunity at all? Am I looking at a job loss? What is the probability of it happening? What is the timeline we are looking at? How would my family react to such an event happening? How would I deal the situation with my extended family, friends? The outside situation was grim too. There was no clarity about anything. The anxiety levels were rising as the days go by, with seemingly no answers anywhere close to be found.

Best way to cope with and bring certainty about uncertainty is to clearly identify & define "What is that we can control?" and "What is beyond us?"

Applying the same technique, To solve the riddle in front of me, what I could control was:

- Reach out to my manager to understand clearly:
- What opportunities are visible to him which I could pursue?
- What feedback if any he got from my earlier interviews?
- What can I do differently in pursuing future opportunities?
- What is the probability of impending "layoff" happening?
- What is the timeline that from an organization perspective we are looking at?

Getting answers to these questions gave me lot of clarity, also probability of the worst case scenario occurring and also tentative timelines to look at. Did it bring down the uncertainty, I say yes, to a great extent. What I used here was the courage to ask the questions which I know should be asked but what stopped me was the fear of facing the reality. The more we run away from the reality, the more anxious and desperate we become.

What we questions we could answer when we are facing job loss:

- What's our current financial state in terms of assets & liabilities?

- What's the duration for which I have built sustenance for?
- what expenses can I avoid, to bringdown my liabilities further?
- What's the minimum amount of expenses I need to fulfil on monthly basis?

Bringing certainty to financial situation we are in and clarity around the needs & what should be cut down to manage the situation can give us lot of clarity on the sense of urgency we have around ourselves.

What else could cause uncertainty in our lives:

- Potential possibility of a job loss
- Losing a job
- Losing our bread winner
- Failing a critical examination
- Failing to get acceptance of your love
- Break up in a relationship
- Betrayal
- Pandemic
- Losing immediate family

All the above events can throw us into the world of uncertainty. This is not an exhaustive list and there could be many more.

Below are the steps to be certain about the uncertainty:

- Define clearly What's in our control, and the rest is beyond us
- Define what's the best & worst case scenarios
- Identify the probability of occurrence
- Identify the timelines for the event to occur

Now that we are certain about what we can control and what is uncertain, let's move ahead into step 2.

STEP 2: ANALYSE THE IMPACT

The second step in the framework is analyse the impact. This should not be restricted to just financial impact but should cover social, reputational & relationship impacts too. Having a visibility around these helps us to enhance our awareness about our situation, alters our expectations on how people in & around us would treat us and increases our acceptance levels of any change in their behaviours towards us. The impact will not be just to ourselves but will also be extended to our immediate family members too.

"Never regret. If it's good, it's wonderful. If it's bad, it's experience"
- Victoria Holt

What we need to look into when we are faced with a job loss is our book of expenses. In general, when we have money landing in our accounts at the end of every month, seldom do we worry about how we are spending our money. The expenses are more natural and many times uncalled for. There are very few people that I personally have come across who have complete hang of their day to day expenses. But this needs to change when we are faced with a job loss or a potential job loss. It's time for us to sit with our partners, Spouse & kids (if grown up) to transparently have an open conversation about the impending situation.

- List out all the expenses & liabilities that we have today.
- Start striking out all the optional ones, to arrive at our mandatory expenses which we can't do away with.
- What are the savings (corpus) that we have in our kitty, on which we have to plan our sustenance till we find our next opportunity?
- What are the assets that we can dispose off, to reduce our liabilities & increase our sustenance?(if we don't find our next opportunity soon enough)
- What's the duration that we can sustain with the current assets & liabilities?

-

Answering the above questions gives us good clarity about the financial implications of the job loss we are faced with. Our changing financial situation might or can lead to the relational, social & reputational impacts. These coupled with financial impact influence our mental & emotional health conditions. This is where the personality traits we addressed earlier come into play and help us navigate through the situation.

"A problem well defined is a problem half solved", by defining the uncertainty and analysing the impact it would create, we would have clearly defined the problem we are faced with. This would definitely reduce our anxiety levels as we are now fully aware of the current state, else we would still be questioning ourselves about "Why this happened to me?" or "Why am I the chosen one?" or "I don't know what hit me" etc.
Our thought process now shifts from being worried about the problem.

"Why did it happen to me" to "What we can do about it?"

STEP 3: VISUALISE YOUR STRENGTHS

The third step in the framework is to know ourselves better, identify our strengths, how they have helped us come this far and how we can use them further in our journey to Bounce Back.

"Know your strengths & take advantage of them" - Greg Norman

When we are disrupted, our thoughts are focused on what we don't have (branding, financial backup, a good network etc) or what we lack (technical, functional, domain skills etc)or what we didn't learn (emerging technologies, leadership skills, ways of working etc) which is making us not being in demand in the job market.

Focusing on all these when we are disrupted, only increases negativity in our lives and brings down our energy & motivation levels. However, the time to focus on these is not when we are in state of desperation but when we are actually in a state of comfort or when we are successful. The time is now to focus on our strengths. How do we do that?

One way is to ask for specific feedback from the group of people whom you can trust and have confidence in. Be specific about what you want feedback on. Once you receive the feedback, put them in the four magic quadrants below based on where they belong.

Strengths that I know I have & others know too

Known Strengths

Strengths that I know I have & but others don't know

Hidden Strengths

Unknown Unknowns

Strengths that I don't know I have & but others know

Blind Spots

Strengths that I don't know I have & but others know

We can then segment these into our skills, personality traits, behaviours, habits etc.

- Known Strengths: These are strengths that we know we have, are exhibiting prominently in our daily life and are notices by everyone around us.
- Hidden Strengths: These are strengths that we know we have, we think we are exhibiting in our daily life but are noticed by people around us or we are not exhibiting them enough for others to notice. These reflect our underutilised strengths and contribute to unrealised potential.
- Blind Spots: These are strengths that we don't know we have, but others think we are exhibiting in our daily life and are noticed by people around us. These reflect our blind spots & consciously un-utilised strengths and also contribute to unrealised potential.
  The other way is:
- List down all significant successes we have accomplished so far in life.

- List down all set of actions we have taken that helped us in accomplishing those.
- List down what roadblocks we faced and how we overcame those in our journey.
- Then start listing out what skills, beliefs, behaviours, habits helped us in our pursuit of those objectives.
- Validate those with our trusted partners to seek their feedback and observations.
- Add/modify the list based on their observations & feedback

Following either of the two above options, we would now have not just visualised our strengths but also how we potentially used them to accomplish what we have.

STEP 4: IDENTIFY POSSIBILITIES

While it is important for us to understand the impact from the Uncertainty, fears driving it and the constraints, it's important to move towards identifying what opportunities / possibilities that we can take advantage of using our own strengths, capabilities and the strength of our relationship with trusted people in our sphere of influence. This helps us a great deal in developing a positive perspective to the situation we are facing.

For this to happen, One of the most important things that one can do when presented with a challenging situation is to find reasons to be hopeful. If you are struggling, don't just give up. Finding the silver lining in every cloud will make for a more positive outlook.

The five steps to identifying an opportunity:

- **Find a problem that needs solving:** There are plenty of problems in the world that need solving, and these provide us the opportunity to make a living by finding ways to solve them. List out all the problems that you can visualise which need to be solved.

- **Rank them in order by the level of confidence you have in finding a solution that fits:** Once you have listed out all the problems, start thinking about the solutions that you can provide to resolve them, how practicable they are, how equipped you are, what does it take for you to make it happen.

- **Check for competition in the market:** There could always be solutions that already exist which could potentially be enhanced or modified to solve the problem you are focusing on. If something exists, be sure to analyse and understand the functionalities they have, their value proposition, customer segment they are targeting etc.

- **Define your value proposition:** Now that you are clear about the problem you are looking to solve, the possible solution, what it takes for you to put it out there in the market, who are your nearest competitors, their value proposition and customer segment, you start defining your value proposition that differentiates you from your competition, what's your uniqueness that you are bringing as value to the customers that others don't have based on your knowledge, strengths, experience, expertise, your network etc.

- **Identify if it is a risk worth taking:** This is the most important thing that makes or breaks it. If you are thinking, will this work for me? Then possibly you are not convinced enough. Rather, you should start thinking about how convinced you are that "this is the Opportunity and you are going to do everything to make it work".

If the answer is "YES, I am going to make it work" then that is the opportunity that you want to be embarking next on.

STEP 5: IDENTIFY SUPPORT SYSTEM

Having a support system is crucial for overall well-being. Support systems are groups of people who provide emotional and practical support to one another. A support system can consist of Family, Friends, Co-workers, Mentors, Coaches etc. There are many ways in which you can build a supportive network in your life. It may include joining relevant groups on LinkedIn or Facebook, or it could be walking down the street with someone, or calling a friend or people in your social network up frequently.

Oftentimes, people will say they don't have a support system because they've never really thought about it or made one, but there are lots of ways to get connected to other people and start building up your support system. Think about the people in your life that provide emotional, financial, or physical support. Usually, they are people who would be there for you if you needed them whether you were celebrating or struggling. This includes friends, family members, mentors, teachers, spiritual advisors, and co-workers. Outline how you can identify the strengths of your support system. Also outline what you can do to strengthen that system. If you're having trouble figuring this out, consider talking to someone close to you about where you stand with respect to their support.

How to build a support system?

- **Make your needs known to your close friends and family:** I can tell you from my own personal experience that it helps to have people who believe in you to be there for you. We often neglect our relationships with not just family but our friends too when we are successful and are progressing well in life. But actually that is the time when you need to be nurturing these relationships so you can look up to them for support in times of distress.

- **Seek out groups online that you might find helpful:** In today's society, it is sometimes hard to find support from friends and family. This is especially true when people have mental health conditions or even extreme financial situations that others cannot relate to. In order to ensure that this does not happen, you should seek out groups online that you might find helpful. You can take a look at forums and support groups on social media platforms such as Facebook and Twitter in order to find a community of people you can trust.

- **Reach out to people in the community who might not be close friends or family but can provide support:** It can be difficult to go through tough times by yourself. And even if you have a close-knit group of friends and family, there are sometimes people that seem more distant but can provide support. There are several ways to find out who these people are. One way is to reflect on past events in your life. Who was there for you when things were tough? Who provided support without needing anything in return?

- **Don't give up even when things get tough:** It's easy to get discouraged when life throws you a curveball. However, having a support system is the key to feeling grounded and focused on getting through whatever tough time you are experiencing. We all need someone who understands us, who will listen to our feelings, and who will always be there for us during both happy moments and difficult ones.

The strength of your support system can define how resilient you are and how quickly you can bounce back. It's imperative to nurture our relationships not just with our immediate family and close knit friends but with people beyond that, whether it is with people at work, in your social network or groups that you are involved with.

How strong is your support system?

Steps 6 - 10

STEP 6: DEFINE OPTIONS

In life, there are many different things to focus on especially when things are going down south. There can be some things that take up a lot of your time and energy, while other things might not get as much attention as they deserve. In order to make sure you're focusing on the most important aspects of your life, it's important to prioritize what needs to be addressed first.

So how do you know what should come next? How do you decide which opportunities are more important than others? We all go through this stage at one point or another in our lives. Whether we've been told by parents or teachers, or learned about this from experience; people have always found ways of understanding their priorities in life.

One way of doing so is by using the ABC method, also known as the "ABC model". It was developed by Dr. Abraham Maslow back in 1943.

If you want to learn more about this amazing tool, check out his website – https://positivepsychology.com/albert-ellis-abc-model-rebt-cbt/

The ABC Method provides a simple framework for making decisions in life. It helps us see if something really matters when we face difficult situations, because there never seems to be enough time or energy to pursue all options that we have in front of us. By learning how to use the ABC method, you can figure out what's important in your own personal situation.

Things to consider when prioritising options

When you're faced with a difficult decision, you need to know how to make the right choice. One way to prioritise is to engage in a process called ranking. Ranking involves evaluating the options against three criteria:

- What do I want?
- What needs to be done?
- What's most important?

You then rank them accordingly, giving each option a score of one through three. The first step is to consider what matters most to you. You may already know what's best for yourself. Or maybe you don't and that's why you're asking here!

In any case, think about it very carefully before moving on to the rest of the steps. What's essential, and not so vital? Next, start thinking about actions and activities that will help achieve your objectives. What are your top five choices? Once all these things are clear, work through the remaining items in order of importance.

How to choose between two alternative?

In real-world problems, often there aren't just two choices available but several (e.g., choosing between a new job or taking an old position) or even many (e.g. which college should I go to). This means that we have to decide among more than our usual two choices. A practical rule of thumb is that every extra alternative doubles the complexity of a problem by increasing its number of possible outcomes while at the same time reducing the probability of a perfect outcome.

As such, we must never spend too long pondering over decisions involving more than two options without being sure whether they really offer us useful information. For this reason, ranking makes sense only if we have enough knowledge about the different options under consideration. The best thing to do it to go with what resonates with you the most based on the strengths you have and the probability of it succeeding.

What is your order of priority for the opportunities you have finalised?

STEP 7: DEFINE OBJECTIVES & STRATEGY

Objectives are important for having direction in life, especially when it gets difficult to make decisions. Once you have figured out what opportunities you are going to pursue, the next step is to define the objectives which once achieved will result in make the best of the opportunities identified.

Defining objectives is an important part of the goal-setting process. Without this step, it becomes difficult to know what steps need to be taken to reach the desired outcome or how to measure success. It's also helpful because it forces us to break down the steps so we can better figure out what needs to be done and how long it will take.

The steps to define objectives are similar to the steps for writing goals. The main difference is that with objectives, it's more about what you want to get done. For example, if you want to launch a new training then defining an objective that says something like "Deliver this training to "500" customers within next One Year".

When looking to defining objectives, you mostly are worried about the costs they might bring in. There are quite a few strategies that one can choose where the only thing we need to invest is our effort. These could be bracketed under Active Income sources & Passive Income strategies.

Active Income Sources: These are the sources where you are required to be actively involved at the time of execution, e.g. Conducting Training Classes – whether physically face to face or even virtually, conducting Webinars or workshops etc. You can also look to become a freelancer in your field of expertise. With the pandemic hitting us earlier, most organizations are encouraging remote working which has removed the constraints of people being needed to be located where the work is actually happening. Freelancing also provides you to choose when, and under what conditions you like to undertake work.

Passive Income Sources: These are sources where you can make income by creating learning material and hosting them online for people to go through at their own convenience, e.g. creating courses on Udemy or Coursera or any other digital learning platform or publishing videos on a subscription mode on YouTube channel or streaming pre-recorded sessions through webinar platforms.

If you have expertise in a specific domain and are able to share your knowledge with people to enhance their skillsets, there are big opportunities available that are absolutely free. To create best content, you can use free tools to create your videos like Vimeo, or Loom, or Prezi and for creating great presentations, or eBooks, or workbooks etc, use Canva which provides lot of options even in the free version.

What Objectives have you defined for the prioritised options finalised?

What strategies have you devised for the objectives to be accomplished within the timeframe defined?

STEP 8: DEFINE KEY RESULTS & ACTIONS

Many people have a difficult time measuring their progress and lose their way in life as they can't figure out if they are on track towards what they intended to accomplish. It is important to define a tangible objective and a measurable key result, which together paint the picture of progress.

Objectives are what you hope to achieve by the end of a specific period. Key results are the measurement of those objectives. Without both objectives and key results, it can be hard to measure your success or progress even if it looks as though you're making successful strides towards achieving your goals.

In order to measure your progress and if it is in line with what you intended and you are still aligned to the objectives, you need to define Key Results that will validate your progress. This ensures you clearly understand what you should work towards and provides a roadmap for you in case things move off course during execution and course correct. If you have the right metrics in place, you will be able to determine if you are on target with achieving those objectives. Ideally, you should define 3 key results for each objective and ensure those are quantified and are timeboxed to give you the direction to progress upon. You can find free OKR Templates to use here: https://www.aha.io/roadmapping/guide/templates/okr

Once you have the Objectives & Key Results (OKR) framework setup, the next step is to identify actions. Actions are the set of tasks that are required to be completed for you to be able to achieve the Key Result within the timebox identified. For e.g. If your objective was to "Deliver this training to "500" customers within next One Year", then your Key Results could be, Complete 100 Trainings by the end of first Three Months, Complete 200 Trainings by the end of next Six Months, Complete 350 Trainings by end of next Nine Months. These Key Results help you to make sure you are on track to accomplish your overall objective and device necessary actions to accomplish them.

The actions that can be planned in the current e.g. listed above could be to finalise a training calendar to be published, content curation for the trainings identified, what are the tools required, mode of training (physical / virtual / hybrid), the cost of training, marketing, advertising needed etc. Once all the actions are identified, then you start sequencing the actions, effort involved, define dependencies between the, identify risks, possible options to overcome them, effort involved in completing these actions, resources and support needed.

Defining all these will give you a good execution plan to baseline your efforts on. The more confident you are on your level of planning, the more chances of you committing to the plan and in the end succeeding.

What Key Results will help you validate your progress towards the objectives you have prioritised?

What Initiatives do you need to undertake to accomplish the Key Results?

STEP 9: IMPLEMENT ACTIONS

Actions may look very good and easy on paper, but once you start implementing them is when you start understanding the complexity and gaps in your planning. This is where you need flexibility in our thoughts, mindset and approach which helps you to adapt your plans to changing environment that you are implementing them in. The change may be necessitated by new information evolving out of actions you implemented or new knowledge or even experience gained from the progress made thus far.

Plans should never be written in stone and planning needs to be done just enough for you to accomplish the next key result. This helps you to be flexible naturally and removes the resistance that can originate from having an end to end plan which is extensive and detail oriented.

It is quite possible for you to get distracted or sometimes lose hope when you are doing what you had planned but are not able to see the results you wanted. It's important for you to have few people whom you can reach out to understand why things are not working as you expected them to be and what needs to possibly change.

Once you have laid down a plan, you should really stick to that plan with full motivation, commitment and drive in order to do everything that is needed for you to succeed. There are bound to be gaps that will show up in your planning as not everything we planned would come true. It's about being flexible and be clear of the motivators you started these actions with. You should pursue the actions consistently until unless the results or outcomes indicate either you are off-track or your plans are irrelevant in view of the new information evolving.

If in case you land up in a situation that the plans or objectives or even the opportunity you are pursuing is no longer relevant due to whatever reasons, you will need to go back to STEP 4, Identifying Possibilities.

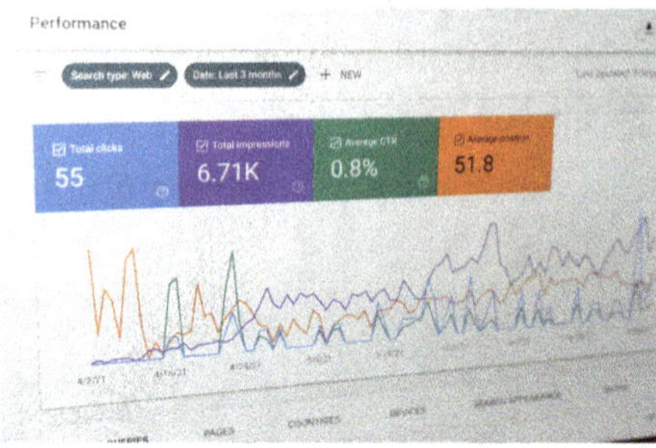

STEP 10: VALIDATE OUTCOMES

Validating outcomes can be a difficult task because in order to validate an outcome, it must be compared against what was originally expected in order to know how successful it has been. It is often easy to suggest that something needs to be improved or done differently when there is no truthful comparison. The more clear your Objectives & Key Results are, the more easier it is for you to validate your progress of where you are and how you need to progress.

Validating is a necessary step in evaluating whether or not we are measuring the right things. As such, there is no set frequency for validating. Instead, it depends on the type of data you collect and how often it changes over time. This is important because invalid data can lead to misleading results and faulty conclusions. For example, if your validation frequency is too high, then you may lose some granularity in your analysis and may miss details or nuances in trends. Meanwhile, if you don't validate enough, you could run into problems with statistical significance (i.e., making incorrect assumptions). Depending on the Objectives & Key Results you have defined, you will need to determine the frequency of validation as what is appropriate by balancing these two factors.

If you don't validate your outcomes and have not set the right frequency, it is quite possible that you will progress on a path that is quite different to what you should ideally be pursuing without realising the need for course correction. This can lead to two different things, you may end up accomplishing something which you have not set out for (can turn out to be positive too) or may lead to loss of a large effort which can be demotivating enough for you to stop pursuing the opportunity.

It is a herculean task to get back your motivation levels up and running again and you have to follow the whole process of bouncing back right from the beginning which is a test of your resilience and willingness to make a difference to yourself.

Irrespective of the level of distress in your life, the amount of difficulties you have, it is always possible to bounce back. It's all about looking at every challenge that is thrown at us by life as an opportunity to grow yourself as an individual and contribute your bit to the betterment of the society by finding problems that you can solve not just for yourself but for a larger section of the community.

It's easier to lose hope, feel left out of the race but it is important to understand that the only person you are racing against and should be racing against in life is only "YOU".

The journey of life is always about being the better version of yourself than you were yesterday and the only person who can stop you from being on that journey is yourself. So,

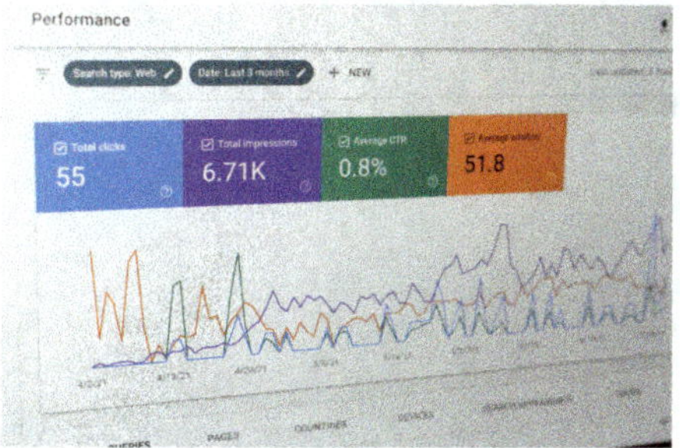

Performance
Search type: Web
Date: Last 3 months
+ NEW
Total clicks
55
Total impressions
6.71K
Average CTR
0.8%
Average position
51.8

References

David, Susan. *Emotional Agility.*

Duhigg, Charles. *The Power of Habit.*

McLaren, Karla. *The Art of Empathy: A Complete Guide to Life's Most Essential Skill.*

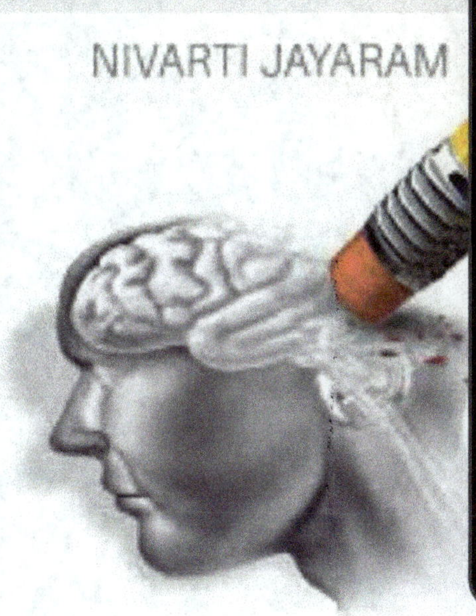

NIVARTI JAYARAM
UNLEARNING
THE SECRET TO
BETTER COACHING ENGAGEMENTS

NIVARTI JAYARAM
UNLEARNING
THE SECRET TO
BETTER COACHING ENGAGEMENTS

Do it yourself
Workbook

4

THE WORKBOOK

Q1. What is the Uncertainty?

Q2. What is causing the Uncertainty?

Q3. How is the Uncertainty impacting you?

Q4. What could be the worst outcome from the Uncertainty?

Q5. What is the probability of it occurring?

Q6. What could be the impact of the worst-case scenario?

Q7. What do you fear most about the worst-case scenario?

Q8. What beliefs of yours are driving those fears?

Q9. What assumptions are you making?

Q10. How can you validate those assumptions?

Q11. What is causing the Uncertainty?

Q12. What is your level of acceptance of the situation?

Q13. What needs to change for you to accept the reality as is?

Q14. What are the dependencies /liabilities that you need to fulfil?

Q15. What expectations you need to manage to bring down the level of Uncertainty?

Q16. Who are the critical stakeholders whose expectations need to be managed?

Q17. What actions can you take to set their expectations right?

Q18. What can come in your way of taking those actions?

Q19. What support would you need to overcome those?

Q20. Who are the critiques that you are most worried about?

Q21. How would their criticism impact or influence you?

Q22. How will their criticism serve you in managing the Uncertainty?

Q23. How do you think you should handle that criticism to better manage the Uncertainty?

Q24. What plans do you have in place for sustenance today?

Q25. What other possibilities can you visualise that can help you meet your needs / liabilities?

Q26. What strengths of yours can help you to realise these possibilities?

Q27. What credibility you have built which can help you in maximising success?

Q28. What actions do you think you need to commit to, for realising the possibilities?

Q29. What key results will you accomplish from completing these actions?

Q30. What can come in your way of taking these actions?

Q31. What support / resources would you need to overcome those?

Q32. Who are your trusted partners that you can look up for support?

Q33. What support are you expecting from them?

Q34. How would you reach out to them for support?

Q35. What would their support change for you?

Q36. Who else can you reach out if in case you don't get support from those you expected?

Q37. What other actions would you need to undertake if you don't get the support expected?

Q38. What is the level of Uncertainty with what you have reflected upon so far?

Q39. How committed you are about taking all the identified actions in managing the Uncertainty and bouncing back?

Q40. What's the level of confidence you have about managing the Uncertainty and bouncing back?

Q41. What other questions if we had asked would have helped you to be in a better state to manage the Uncertainty and Bounce Back?

Q42. What would your answer to those questions be?

Q43. How would that help you enhance your ability to Bounce Back?

Q44. WHAT HAVE YOU LEARNT ABOUT YOURSELF ANSWERING ALL THESE QUESTIONS?

"Challenge the status quo and continuous self-discovery through Unlearning" is what I strongly believe in and it helps me in extending my horizons. I have published a book on Unlearning that outlines the various aspects of Unlearning and its significance in personal or organizational transformation journey.

Certified Executive & Leadership Coach, Author, Global Speaker, Mentor, Service Veteran, and UN Peacekeeper, I believe agility is a state of mind, and transformation is never a destination, but a continuous and an ongoing journey.

I promote a culture of "being dispensable" through identifying the right talent and building capability to create sustainability in organizations. I am passionate about people and about helping them in enhancing their self-awareness and presence so that they can identify and realize their full potential.

I am an expert at Enterprise Transformation, covering people, products, processes, and technology, helping them to not just survive but thrive & excel in the VUCA (Volatile, Uncertain, Complex, Ambiguous) world.

If you would like to know more about me, log on to:

www.nivartijayaram.com
https://www.linkedin.com/in/nivartijayaram